GOD'S BLUEPRINT FOR SPIRITUAL HEALTH

How the Bible Knows Your Soul

Jordan Schneider

Copyright © 2025 All Rights Reserved

Copyright © 2025. No portion of this book may be reproduced, stored in a retrieval system, or transmitted in any form or by any means—electronic, mechanical, photocopying, recording, or otherwise—without the express written permission of the publisher, except for brief quotations used in articles, reviews, or academic works.

This publication is designed to provide scriptural and educational insight and is not intended as a substitute for medical or psychological treatment. Readers should seek guidance from qualified professionals for personal health concerns.

Unless otherwise noted, all Scripture references are taken from the King James Version (KJV) of the Bible, which is in the public domain.

Title: God's Blueprint for Spiritual Health: How the Bible Knows Your Soul
Author: Jordan Schneider
Publisher: Jordan Schneider
Editor: Giselle Valdes
Printed in the United States of America
First Edition – 2025

For permissions, inquiries, or bulk orders, please contact: Gbpfh@yahoo.com

To those who are searching, questioning, or longing for something more—may you find the hope, peace, and purpose that can only be found in Jesus Christ.

"And the very God of peace sanctify you wholly; and I pray God your whole spirit and soul and body be preserved blameless unto the coming of our Lord Jesus Christ."

1 THESSALONIANS 5:23, KJV

CONTENTS

- Title Page
- Copyright
- Dedication
- Epigraph
- Preface
- Prologue
- Prayer of Encouragement
- Introduction: The Divine Blueprint for the Soul
- Chapter 1: What is the Soul? The Bible's Definition vs. Science
- Chapter 1 Practical Applications for the Soul
- Chapter 2: Spiritual Malnutrition – What Harms the Soul?
- Chapter 2 Practical Applications to Heal and Protect the Soul
- Chapter 3: The Power of Prayer and Meditation on the Soul
- Chapter 3 Practical Applications to Strengthen the Soul Through Prayer
- Chapter 4: The Transformative Power of Scripture on the Soul
- Chapter 4 Practical Applications to Transform the Soul Through Scripture
- Chapter 5: The Role of Community and Worship in Spiritual Health
- Chapter 5 Practical Applications to Strengthen Your Soul Through Community and Worship
- Chapter 6: Forgiveness and Its Power Over the Soul
- Chapter 6 Practical Applications to Heal Through Forgiveness
- Chapter 7: The Impact of Gratitude and Joy on Spiritual Health
- Chapter 7 Practical Applications to Cultivate Gratitude and Joy
- Chapter 8: Spiritual Warfare – Protecting the Soul
- Chapter 8 Practical Applications to Protect the Soul in Spiritual Warfare
- Chapter 9: Death, Eternity, and the Soul's Final Destination

Chapter 9 Practical Applications to Live with an Eternal Perspective

Chapter 10: The Dangers of Bitterness and Resentment

Chapter 10 Practical Applications to Uproot Bitterness

Chapter 11: The Power of Hope and Purpose

Chapter 11 Practical Applications to Cultivate Hope and Purpose

Chapter 12: Rest for the Soul – The Sabbath and Sleep

Chapter 12 Practical Applications to Restore the Soul Through Rest

Chapter 13: Humility vs. Pride – The Mental Health Consequences

Chapter 13 Practical Applications to Cultivate Humility and Defeat Pride

Chapter 14: The Healing Power of Service and Compassion

Chapter 14 Practical Applications to Heal Through Service and Compassion

Chapter 15: Identity in Christ vs. Identity Crisis

Chapter 15 Practical Applications to Root Identity in Christ

Chapter 16: The Weight of Shame vs. the Freedom of Grace

Chapter 16 Practical Applications to Break Free from Shame

Chapter 17: The Healing Power of Confession and Honesty

Chapter 17 Practical Applications to Free the Soul Through Confession

Chapter 18: The Strength Found in Surrender and Trust

Chapter 18 Practical Applications to Strengthen the Soul Through Surrender

Chapter 19: The Peace that Comes from Obedience

Chapter 19 Practical Applications to Anchor the Soul THrough Obedience

Chapter 20: The Soul's Need for Wonder and Worship

Chapter 20 Practical Applications to Awaken the Soul Through Worship and Awe

Conclusion: Aligning with God's Blueprint for Spiritual Health

Call to Faith: A Personal Invitation to Receive Jesus Christ

Salvation Prayer

Support this ministry

About The Author

[Books By This Author](#)

PREFACE

The soul is the most precious part of who we are—yet in today's world, it's the most overlooked.

We talk freely about physical health, mental health, and emotional wellness, but rarely do we speak about the condition of the soul. And yet, all other forms of health flow from it. A neglected soul leads to a restless mind, a weary heart, and a confused identity. But a soul that is rooted in God's truth is steady, peaceful, and full of life—even in the middle of chaos.

This book was born from a desire to bridge the gap between biblical truth and modern understanding. As someone who deeply values both Scripture and the study of the mind, I've watched with awe as scientific discoveries continue to confirm what the Bible has said all along. The world is only just now uncovering what God declared thousands of years ago about peace, forgiveness, identity, joy, and healing. And that alignment is no coincidence—it's divine authorship.

God's Blueprint for Spiritual Health is not just a guide for personal well-being. It's an invitation to return to the One who created your soul and knows exactly how to restore it. Each chapter is crafted to be both deeply biblical and practically useful, blending King James Scripture with current research, and ending with actionable steps you can take to nurture your inner life.

My prayer is that this book would do more than educate—it would transform. That you wouldn't just learn about spiritual health, but experience it. And more importantly, that you would come to know the Healer of the soul: Jesus Christ.

May you read with openness, reflect with honesty, and walk away with renewed hope.

—Jordan Schneider

PROLOGUE

The soul is invisible, yet undeniable. You can't scan it in an MRI, and you can't locate it on a map—but you know when it's hurting. You feel it when you're alone in the dark, when your heart is heavy, when you long for peace and can't explain why it's missing. You sense it when joy floods in, when beauty moves you to tears, or when conviction grips you deep inside. That's your soul—crying out, reaching upward, longing for what it was made for.

From the beginning, God created man not merely as a body or a mind, but as a living soul. And from that moment on, the condition of the soul has determined the direction of every life and every generation.

Today, our world is drowning in anxiety, identity confusion, fear, and emotional exhaustion. People are searching—through self-help, therapy, mindfulness, or distraction. And while many of these methods offer temporary relief, none of them fully satisfy the soul. Because only the One who made the soul knows how to heal it.

This book is not about religion. It's about restoration. It's about how the Word of God—written thousands of years ago—perfectly diagnoses and heals the deepest needs of the human heart. It's about how the Bible has always known the path to peace, purpose, and freedom. And it's about how modern science is finally beginning to catch up.

What you're about to read is more than information. It's a blueprint. A divine design for soul health that leads not only to emotional wellness—but to eternal life.

The journey begins here.

PRAYER OF ENCOURAGEMENT

◆ ◆ ◆

Lord, we come before You with open hearts, asking that You speak through these words. May this book not just be information, but transformation.

For every reader, may Your truth take root, bringing conviction, healing, and renewed faith. Let this be a tool for your glory and an instrument of Your love.

In Jesus' name, Amen.

INTRODUCTION: THE DIVINE BLUEPRINT FOR THE SOUL

♦ ♦ ♦

For thousands of years, humanity has pondered the nature of the soul. What is it? Where does it come from? What happens to it after we die? These questions have captured the curiosity of philosophers, theologians, and scientists alike. While modern research continues to explore consciousness, identity, and purpose, the Bible has held the answers all along.

Written over centuries by more than 40 human authors on three continents —yet united in one central message—the Bible boldly speaks of the soul's origin, nature, and destiny. Its words are not the product of human imagination but of divine revelation. As 2 Timothy 3:16 (KJV) declares, "All scripture is given by inspiration of God, and is profitable for doctrine, for reproof, for correction, for instruction in righteousness."

What's even more remarkable is that modern scientific discoveries are only beginning to catch up with what Scripture revealed thousands of years ago. This book will explore how the Bible, without the aid of modern medicine, psychology, or neuroscience, outlines a flawless guide to spiritual health— what we're calling God's blueprint.

Whether addressing anxiety, guilt, joy, identity, or the need for rest and connection, the Bible's teachings are not only spiritually profound but also medically sound. The alignment between ancient Scripture and modern science cannot be explained by coincidence—it points directly to divine authorship. These are not outdated religious ideas; they are timeless truths authored by the Creator of the human soul.

In this book, we will examine how aligning our lives with biblical wisdom leads to a thriving soul. Each chapter will explore a specific aspect of spiritual health, reveal what the Bible says about it, and compare those insights with current scientific understanding. The goal is not only to highlight the Bible's brilliance, but to provide practical steps for healing, growth, and transformation—spiritually and psychologically.

We'll uncover how prayer reshapes the brain, how forgiveness frees us emotionally, how gratitude improves our health, and how Scripture restores our identity. And at every turn, we'll see that the Bible didn't just know about these truths—it knew how to apply them.

More importantly, this book is not just about personal wellness. The ultimate purpose of the Bible is not to make us feel better temporarily, but to lead us to eternal life. The same God who created your soul also sent His Son, Jesus Christ, to redeem it. The Bible is God's message to humanity—not just for flourishing in this life, but for salvation in the life to come.

CHAPTER 1: WHAT IS THE SOUL? THE BIBLE'S DEFINITION VS. SCIENCE

◆ ◆ ◆

What exactly is the soul? The word is often used in religious contexts, but its meaning is often misunderstood or dismissed by modern culture. Yet the Bible speaks of the soul not as a poetic idea, but as a real, eternal part of who we are—distinct from the body and the spirit. According to Scripture, your soul is the very core of your identity, your emotions, your will, your mind, and your moral consciousness.

"And the LORD God formed man of the dust of the ground, and breathed into his nostrils the breath of life; and man became a living soul." (Genesis 2:7, KJV)

This verse reveals something powerful: when God created man, it wasn't the body alone that defined humanity. The human soul came to life when God Himself breathed life into the body. Your soul is the breath of God made personal—an eternal part of your being that cannot be touched by physical death.

The Soul is Eternal

"Fear not them which kill the body, but are not able to kill the soul: but rather fear him which is able to destroy both soul and body in hell." (Matthew 10:28, KJV)

Jesus taught that while the body can be harmed or even destroyed, the soul endures. It is the part of you that connects to God, can be redeemed by grace, or lost in separation from Him. This truth sets the soul apart from the brain or mind—it is not simply an electrical pattern in your nervous system. It is the true, eternal you.

Science is Catching Up

For centuries, science dismissed the soul as untestable. But in recent decades, the scientific community has been forced to acknowledge phenomena it cannot fully explain:

Consciousness: Despite all advances in neuroscience, no scientist can explain how or why we are aware of ourselves. This self-awareness is central to the biblical view of the soul.

Near-Death Experiences: Thousands of documented cases reveal people who were clinically dead yet reported vivid experiences, thoughts, and emotions—often with spiritual clarity. These events support the Bible's claim that life continues beyond the body.

Moral Reasoning: Human beings have a deeply embedded moral compass. Even toddlers show signs of justice, empathy, and fairness. This echoes what Romans 2:15 teaches—that the law of God is written on the heart.

"Which shew the work of the law written in their hearts, their conscience also bearing witness…" (Romans 2:15, KJV)

Scientific studies on human behavior, emotion, and consciousness continually circle back to what Scripture has always taught: we are more than matter. We are souls.

Why This Matters

If you don't understand what the soul is, you can't care for it. In today's world, people are quick to treat mental health, physical health, and emotional health—but neglect the soul entirely. This neglect leads to a sense of emptiness, restlessness, and confusion that can't be fixed with medicine or therapy alone. Spiritual sickness needs a spiritual remedy.

The Bible calls us to tend to our souls—to know God, seek His truth, and align ourselves with His will. Only then do we experience true peace and flourishing.

CHAPTER 1 PRACTICAL APPLICATIONS FOR THE SOUL

♦ ♦ ♦

Biblical Applications:

1. Read Scripture Daily – Feed your soul with the Word of God (Matthew 4:4).

2. Spend Time in Prayer – Talk to God honestly, building your spiritual connection (Psalm 62:8).

3. Guard Your Heart and Mind – Be mindful of what you allow into your life (Proverbs 4:23).

4. Worship God Regularly – Worship aligns your soul with its Creator (Psalm 103:1).

Medical & Scientific Applications:

1. Practice Daily Reflection or Journaling – Enhances self-awareness and strengthens identity.

2. Spend Time in Nature – Proven to reduce anxiety and increase a sense of spiritual well-being.

3. Connect with Meaningful Communities – Belonging and purpose are vital for soul health.

4. Engage in Mindful Silence – Science confirms even brief periods of silence restore emotional clarity (aligns with biblical meditation, Psalm 46:10).

CHAPTER 2: SPIRITUAL MALNUTRITION – WHAT HARMS THE SOUL?

◆ ◆ ◆

We know what happens to the body when it's deprived of proper nutrition: it weakens, becomes prone to disease, and eventually shuts down. The same is true of the soul. When the soul is deprived of God's truth, presence, and purpose, it becomes malnourished—and the effects are just as real and devastating.

"There is a way which seemeth right unto a man, but the end thereof are the ways of death." (Proverbs 14:12, KJV)

Spiritual malnutrition happens slowly, subtly. It begins when we ignore God's Word, isolate ourselves from community, indulge in sin, or chase after things that may feel good temporarily but leave us empty inside. Eventually, we find ourselves spiritually weak, emotionally unstable, and disconnected from the very One who sustains us.

Sin: The Root of Soul-Starvation

The Bible clearly teaches that sin separates us from God—the source of life for the soul.

"For to be carnally minded is death; but to be spiritually minded is life and peace." (Romans 8:6, KJV)

Carnal living—chasing pleasure, power, or self without God—leads to spiritual death. When we live outside of God's design, we suffer inner decay. Our soul becomes like a tree cut off from its roots: still standing, but slowly dying.

Jesus described this condition when He said:

"Man shall not live by bread alone, but by every word that proceedeth out of the mouth of God." (Matthew 4:4, KJV)

Just as our bodies need food, our souls need God's Word. Without it, we're spiritually starving.

Modern Signs of Spiritual Malnutrition

Science is beginning to recognize the link between spiritual neglect and mental health struggles:

Depression and anxiety often increase when people feel disconnected from meaning, purpose, or moral clarity.

A 2020 study published in Frontiers in Psychology found that individuals who engage in regular spiritual practices—such as prayer, Scripture reading, or worship—report significantly better emotional well-being and lower levels of stress and despair.

People who prioritize spiritual values and live by clear moral convictions tend to experience stronger resilience, even in trauma.

These findings confirm what Scripture has always taught: the soul thrives when it's fed, and withers when neglected.

"My people are destroyed for lack of knowledge." (Hosea 4:6, KJV)

A soul without God's truth is like a ship without a compass—it may float for a while, but it's destined to drift into darkness.

What Feeds the Soul?

Philippians 4:8 gives us a clear filter for what we should allow into our hearts and minds:

"Whatsoever things are true… honest… just… pure… lovely… of good report… think on these things." (Philippians 4:8, KJV)

Whatever we dwell on shapes our soul. Negative media, immoral entertainment, toxic relationships, and godless worldviews do more damage than we realize. We must be intentional about what we feed on—mentally, emotionally, and spiritually.

CHAPTER 2 PRACTICAL APPLICATIONS TO HEAL AND PROTECT THE SOUL

♦ ♦ ♦

Biblical Applications:

1. Confess and Repent of Sin – Spiritual healing begins with humility and honesty (1 John 1:9).

2. Read the Bible as Daily Bread – Feed your soul every day with truth (Jeremiah 15:16).

3. Fast from Harmful Influences – Remove content or activities that poison your spirit (Psalm 101:3).

4. Surround Yourself with Godly People – Community is a key source of strength (Proverbs 13:20).

Medical & Scientific Applications:

1. Establish Purpose-Driven Routines – Purpose provides emotional structure and stability.

2. Limit Media Exposure – Studies show overconsumption of negative media increases stress and depression.

3. Engage in Spiritual Journaling – Reflecting on Scripture or prayer helps regulate emotions.

4. Get Sunlight and Movement – Natural light and physical activity elevate mood and reduce mental fog—both of which affect the soul's vitality.

CHAPTER 3: THE POWER OF PRAYER AND MEDITATION ON THE SOUL

◆ ◆ ◆

In our noisy, chaotic world, the soul longs for stillness, connection, and peace. God has provided a way to access those things—prayer and meditation on His Word. These aren't religious rituals to be rushed through or recited without thought. They are deeply powerful spiritual disciplines that nourish the soul and reshape the mind.

"Be careful for nothing; but in every thing by prayer and supplication with thanksgiving let your requests be made known unto God. And the peace of God, which passeth all understanding, shall keep your hearts and minds through Christ Jesus." (Philippians 4:6–7, KJV)

Prayer is conversation with God, and it leads to peace that surpasses human understanding. It calms the heart, realigns the mind, and strengthens the soul.

The Brain on Prayer

Modern science has caught up with this ancient truth. Studies in neuroscience show that prayer and biblical meditation:

Reduce stress and anxiety

Lower blood pressure and heart rate

Improve emotional regulation

Activate brain regions responsible for empathy and self-control

A 2009 study published in The Southern Medical Journal found that individuals who prayed regularly had lower levels of psychological distress and a stronger sense of purpose. Another study from Columbia University using MRI scans revealed that people who practiced daily prayer showed increased activity in the prefrontal cortex—the area of the brain associated with decision-making, focus, and compassion.

"Thou wilt keep him in perfect peace, whose mind is stayed on thee: because he trusteth in thee." (Isaiah 26:3, KJV)

Prayer literally rewires the mind to reflect the peace and stability of God. This is not self-help; it is soul-help.

Biblical Meditation vs. Secular Mindfulness

Secular meditation teaches people to "empty their minds." But biblical meditation is the opposite—it teaches us to fill our minds with God's truth.

"But his delight is in the law of the LORD; and in his law doth he meditate day and night." (Psalm 1:2, KJV)

Meditation in Scripture means to dwell on God's Word, to repeat it, absorb it, and let it reshape your thoughts. When we meditate on Scripture, we invite God's wisdom into our daily decisions, emotions, and perspectives.

Gratitude and Prayer Activate the Same Brain Center

Here's a powerful truth—science has confirmed that the part of the brain that activates during gratitude is the same region that lights up during anxiety. And here's the catch: you can't experience both at the same time. This explains why the Bible emphasizes gratitude in prayer:

"In every thing give thanks: for this is the will of God in Christ Jesus concerning you." (1 Thessalonians 5:18, KJV)

Practicing thankful prayer is not just a spiritual command—it's a scientifically proven path to peace. The Bible knew this all along.

CHAPTER 3 PRACTICAL APPLICATIONS TO STRENGTHEN THE SOUL THROUGH PRAYER

♦ ♦ ♦

Biblical Applications:

1. Start Each Day with Prayer – Invite God to lead your mind and heart (Psalm 5:3).

2. Keep a Gratitude Prayer List – Praise God regularly for His blessings (Psalm 103:2).

3. Meditate on Scripture – Choose a verse and reflect deeply on its meaning (Joshua 1:8).

4. Pray Honestly and Often – God desires real, heartfelt conversation (Psalm 62:8).

Medical & Scientific Applications:

1. Establish a Quiet Time Routine – Even 10 minutes of prayer or Scripture reading improves mental clarity.

2. Use Breath Prayers – Combining slow breathing with short prayers helps regulate stress and heart rate.

3. Write Your Prayers or Verses – Journaling boosts emotional processing and cognitive focus.

4. Replace Rumination with Meditation – When anxiety strikes, pause to reflect on a promise of God.

CHAPTER 4: THE TRANSFORMATIVE POWER OF SCRIPTURE ON THE SOUL

◆ ◆ ◆

The Bible is more than a book—it is God's living Word, and it has the power to radically transform the human soul. From Genesis to Revelation, it reveals who God is, who we are, and how we can be restored to Him. The words of Scripture aren't just for religious instruction; they are nourishment, healing, and strength for the soul.

"Man shall not live by bread alone, but by every word that proceedeth out of the mouth of God." (Matthew 4:4, KJV)

Just as food sustains the body, the Word of God sustains the soul. Without it, we are spiritually starved. But with it, we are strengthened, renewed, and guided in truth.

Scripture Renews the Mind

"And be not conformed to this world: but be ye transformed by the renewing of your mind, that ye may prove what is that good, and acceptable, and perfect, will of God." (Romans 12:2, KJV)

This verse highlights one of the most powerful truths in Scripture: our minds can be renewed. We do not have to remain stuck in fear, negativity, shame, or confusion. The Word of God rewires our thinking, helps us discern truth, and brings peace and clarity.

Cognitive Behavioral Therapy and the Bible

Modern psychology confirms what the Bible has taught for millennia. Cognitive Behavioral Therapy (CBT)—one of the most effective therapies for anxiety and depression—teaches people to challenge false beliefs, reframe negative thoughts, and replace them with truth.

That is exactly what Scripture has taught all along.

Philippians 4:8 urges us to focus on things that are true, pure, and praiseworthy.

2 Corinthians 10:5 commands us to "cast down imaginations, and every high thing that exalteth itself against the knowledge of God," and to "bring into captivity every thought to the obedience of Christ."

CBT may be new to science, but it's ancient in Scripture. The Bible knew the human mind and how to heal it—because it was authored by the One who created it.

Scripture Gives Identity and Purpose

In a culture of confusion, Scripture offers clarity. We are not defined by our feelings, past mistakes, or what others say. We are defined by God.

"Therefore if any man be in Christ, he is a new creature: old things are passed away; behold, all things are become new." (2 Corinthians 5:17, KJV)

The soul finds rest when it knows who it belongs to and why it exists. The Bible tells us we were created by God, for God, and redeemed by Christ. That identity is unshakeable.

CHAPTER 4 PRACTICAL APPLICATIONS TO TRANSFORM THE SOUL THROUGH SCRIPTURE

◆ ◆ ◆

Biblical Applications:

1. Read the Word Daily – Make Scripture your spiritual food (Job 23:12).

2. Memorize Key Verses – Carry truth with you to fight lies and fear (Psalm 119:11).

3. Use Scripture to Speak Life – Declare God's promises out loud (Proverbs 18:21).

4. Ask God for Revelation – Pray for the Holy Spirit to help you understand (John 14:26).

Medical & Scientific Applications:

1. Practice Thought Replacement – Replace negative self-talk with Scripture (mirrors CBT).

2. Keep a "Truth Journal" – Write down toxic thoughts and challenge them with God's Word.

3. Use Affirmation Cards with Scripture – Repeating truth can reshape thought patterns.

4. Listen to the Bible Audio – Hearing Scripture daily improves focus and mood.

CHAPTER 5: THE ROLE OF COMMUNITY AND WORSHIP IN SPIRITUAL HEALTH

♦ ♦ ♦

The soul was never meant to thrive in isolation. From the beginning, God designed us for connection—with Himself and with others. Just as the body suffers when separated from oxygen, the soul begins to wither when cut off from fellowship and worship.

"And the LORD God said, It is not good that the man should be alone…" (Genesis 2:18, KJV)

While this verse is often quoted in the context of marriage, the principle goes far deeper. God created us as relational beings. We were made to grow together, bear one another's burdens, and worship side by side.

Biblical Community Heals and Strengthens the Soul

"Two are better than one… For if they fall, the one will lift up his fellow." (Ecclesiastes 4:9–10, KJV)

God commands believers to gather together—not only for learning, but for mutual encouragement and support.

"Not forsaking the assembling of ourselves together, as the manner of some is; but exhorting one another…" (Hebrews 10:25, KJV)

Church, small groups, Christian friendships, and even simple gatherings of prayer are spiritual oxygen to the soul. They allow confession, accountability, shared joy, and worship—each one a soul-strengthening practice.

Science Confirms the Power of Connection

Medical studies agree: social support is one of the most powerful predictors of emotional and physical health. According to research published in the Journal of Health and Social Behavior, people who are part of meaningful communities:

Experience lower rates of depression and anxiety

Recover more quickly from illness and trauma

Live longer, more purpose-filled lives

Have greater emotional resilience

When this community is centered around faith and worship, those benefits increase even more. One study from Duke University found that regular church attendance was associated with greater life satisfaction, reduced mortality risk, and fewer symptoms of depression.

The Healing Power of Worship

Worship isn't just a song—it's a spiritual alignment. When we worship God, we take our eyes off ourselves and lift them to the One who gives life. Worship recalibrates our soul, reminding us who we are and who God is.

"Bless the LORD, O my soul: and all that is within me, bless his holy name." (Psalm 103:1, KJV)

Worship also impacts the body and brain. Studies show that singing—especially in a group—releases endorphins, reduces cortisol (stress hormone), and increases oxytocin, a bonding chemical that promotes trust and peace. Simply put, singing praises can literally lift your soul.

CHAPTER 5 PRACTICAL APPLICATIONS TO STRENGTHEN YOUR SOUL THROUGH COMMUNITY AND WORSHIP

◆ ◆ ◆

Biblical Applications:

1. Join a Bible-believing Church – Engage in weekly worship and teaching (Acts 2:42).

2. Participate in Fellowship – Build friendships with other believers (Proverbs 27:17).

3. Worship with Music Daily – Invite God's presence into your heart (Psalm 100:2).

4. Serve Others in Love – Service creates joy and purpose (Galatians 5:13).

Medical & Scientific Applications:

1. Prioritize Social Connection – Isolation increases risk of depression and cognitive decline.

2. Engage in Group Singing or Worship – Reduces stress and elevates mood.

3. Join Supportive Groups – Faith-based or otherwise, groups promote healing and resilience.

4. Attend Events that Promote Belonging – Community activities strengthen the sense of identity and purpose.

CHAPTER 6: FORGIVENESS AND ITS POWER OVER THE SOUL

◆ ◆ ◆

Few things weigh heavier on the human soul than unforgiveness. Whether it's holding onto the wrongs others have done to us or carrying guilt from our own mistakes, unforgiveness creates spiritual and emotional bondage. It distorts relationships, disrupts peace, and poisons joy. But God, in His mercy, offers a powerful cure—forgiveness.

"Let all bitterness, and wrath, and anger, and clamour, and evil speaking, be put away from you, with all malice: And be ye kind one to another, tenderhearted, forgiving one another, even as God for Christ's sake hath forgiven you." (Ephesians 4:31–32, KJV)

Forgiveness is not just a noble idea—it is a command from God and a powerful key to healing the soul.

Unforgiveness is Toxic

When we refuse to forgive, we trap ourselves in a cycle of pain. Bitterness takes root, and anger simmers just below the surface. Over time, this affects not only our relationships but our health.

"Follow peace with all men… lest any root of bitterness springing up trouble you, and thereby many be defiled." (Hebrews 12:14–15, KJV)

Medical research confirms the truth of Scripture:

A study published in Harvard Women's Health Watch found that forgiveness is linked to lower heart rate, blood pressure, and stress levels.

According to research from Johns Hopkins Medicine, forgiveness improves heart health, boosts immune function, and decreases anxiety and depression.

Chronic anger and resentment increase cortisol and adrenaline, which impair memory, concentration, and emotional regulation.

Simply put: unforgiveness damages the soul and the body. But when we release others—and ourselves—through forgiveness, we set our souls free.

God's Forgiveness Transforms the Soul

Before we can fully forgive others, we must first understand the forgiveness we've received from God.

"If we confess our sins, he is faithful and just to forgive us our sins, and to cleanse us from all unrighteousness." (1 John 1:9, KJV)

The soul experiences deep healing when it accepts God's grace. Guilt and shame lose their power. Peace and renewal take their place. Once you have been forgiven, you are empowered to forgive others—not because they deserve it, but because Christ forgave you.

"And forgive us our debts, as we forgive our debtors." (Matthew 6:12, KJV)

Forgiveness doesn't mean forgetting or pretending nothing happened. It means releasing the right to retaliate, trusting God to be the Judge, and choosing freedom over bondage.

CHAPTER 6 PRACTICAL APPLICATIONS TO HEAL THROUGH FORGIVENESS

◆ ◆ ◆

Biblical Applications:

1. Confess Your Sins to God – Receive His cleansing and forgiveness (Psalm 32:5).

2. Pray for Those Who Hurt You – Release bitterness through prayer (Matthew 5:44).

3. Forgive as Christ Forgave You – Make forgiveness a lifestyle, not a one-time act (Colossians 3:13).

4. Seek Reconciliation Where Possible – If safe and healthy, make peace (Romans 12:18).

Medical & Scientific Applications:

1. Write a Letter You Don't Send – Journaling forgiveness helps release emotional pain.

2. Practice Perspective-Taking – Studies show empathy reduces anger and promotes healing.

3. Engage in Stress-Reduction Techniques – Deep breathing and calming routines reduce physiological effects of resentment.

4. Set Healthy Boundaries – Forgiveness doesn't require ongoing closeness with toxic people; boundaries protect the soul.

CHAPTER 7: THE IMPACT OF GRATITUDE AND JOY ON SPIRITUAL HEALTH

♦ ♦ ♦

Gratitude and joy are not just emotional responses—they are spiritual disciplines that strengthen and protect the soul. In the Bible, giving thanks is more than a suggestion; it's a repeated command that carries transformative power. And joy is more than happiness—it's a deep, God-given strength that carries us through both blessings and battles.

"In every thing give thanks: for this is the will of God in Christ Jesus concerning you." (1 Thessalonians 5:18, KJV)

"The joy of the LORD is your strength." (Nehemiah 8:10, KJV)

These verses reveal two profound truths: gratitude is always God's will, and joy is not a luxury—it's a necessity.

Gratitude Rewires the Brain

Science now affirms what Scripture declared long ago: gratitude is healing.

A study published in Clinical Psychology Review found that gratitude significantly improves overall mental health and reduces symptoms of depression and anxiety.

Research from UC Berkeley's Greater Good Science Center shows that regularly practicing gratitude changes brain activity. It activates the prefrontal cortex (responsible for decision-making and focus) and increases serotonin and dopamine—neurotransmitters that enhance mood and motivation.

The act of expressing gratitude builds emotional resilience and strengthens relationships.

When you thank God, even in hardship, you are practicing a form of spiritual resistance. You're choosing hope over despair, light over darkness, and peace over panic.

"Bless the LORD, O my soul, and forget not all his benefits." (Psalm 103:2, KJV)

David taught his soul to remember the goodness of God. That practice still transforms lives today.

Gratitude and Anxiety Cannot Coexist

Earlier, we touched on a fascinating neurological fact: the same part of the brain that activates anxiety is also responsible for gratitude. But they cannot function at full strength at the same time.

That means when you are focused on giving thanks, it's neurologically impossible to stay in a heightened state of anxiety.

This truth affirms Philippians 4:6–7: "Be careful for nothing; but in every thing by prayer and supplication with thanksgiving let your requests be made known unto God. And the peace of God… shall keep your hearts and minds through Christ Jesus." (Philippians 4:6–7, KJV)

The Bible teaches that thanksgiving leads to peace. Now science confirms it.

Joy is a Spiritual Force

Joy is not tied to circumstances. Biblical joy is rooted in God's presence and promises. It is a deep assurance that God is good, He is with you, and your story is not over.

"Rejoice in the Lord alway: and again I say, Rejoice." (Philippians 4:4, KJV)

Choosing joy—even in trials—builds spiritual endurance, emotional strength, and mental clarity.

CHAPTER 7 PRACTICAL APPLICATIONS TO CULTIVATE GRATITUDE AND JOY

◆ ◆ ◆

Biblical Applications:

1. Start Every Prayer with Thanks – Gratitude reorients the soul to God's goodness (Psalm 100:4).

2. Create a Gratitude Journal – Write down daily blessings and answered prayers (Psalm 9:1).

3. Sing Joyful Praise – Worship fuels joy and lifts the soul (Psalm 95:1–2).

4. Focus on the Eternal – Meditate on the joy of your salvation (Luke 10:20).

Medical & Scientific Applications:

1. Daily Gratitude Practice – Write 3 things you're thankful for each day; improves mood and rewires the brain.

2. Savor Small Moments – Practicing mindfulness of joyful moments reduces stress and boosts long-term happiness.

3. Volunteer or Serve Others – Helping others increases joy-producing neurochemicals.

4. Limit Complaints – Reducing negative speech lowers cortisol and improves mental focus.

CHAPTER 8: SPIRITUAL WARFARE – PROTECTING THE SOUL

♦ ♦ ♦

Every soul is in a battle—whether we recognize it or not. The Bible is clear that life on earth involves more than what we can see. Behind anxiety, temptation, confusion, and despair lies an invisible war for your soul. God equips us not only to survive but to overcome.

"For we wrestle not against flesh and blood, but against principalities, against powers, against the rulers of the darkness of this world, against spiritual wickedness in high places." (Ephesians 6:12, KJV)

This is not poetic language. It is a spiritual reality. And yet, through Christ, we are not powerless.

Satan's Strategy: Attack the Mind

The devil's primary battleground is the mind. Just as he deceived Eve in the garden with words, he still seeks to infiltrate the soul through lies, fear, shame, and pride.

"Casting down imaginations, and every high thing that exalteth itself against the knowledge of God, and bringing into captivity every thought to the obedience of Christ." (2 Corinthians 10:5, KJV)

Unchallenged thoughts become strongholds. A stronghold is a mental or emotional pattern that is in rebellion against God's truth. These can include:

Thoughts of worthlessness

Persistent fear and dread

Shame over forgiven sin

Bitterness toward others

Justification of sinful behavior

Each one slowly wears down the soul—unless we learn to fight with God's Word.

Science Confirms the Power of Thought Patterns

Psychology has long studied negative thought loops, which fuel depression, anxiety, and unhealthy behavior. CBT (Cognitive Behavioral Therapy) helps patients recognize and replace irrational beliefs.

This is a clinical version of what Scripture already teaches—renew your mind, take every thought captive, and speak truth.

Brain scans show that chronic fear and anxiety impair memory, decision-making, and emotional regulation.

Conversely, affirming truth, reframing thoughts, and practicing resilience strengthen the brain's pathways for peace and joy.

God's Word equips us with truth that cuts through lies and rewires the soul for victory.

"And ye shall know the truth, and the truth shall make you free." (John 8:32, KJV)

The Armor of God: Your Spiritual Defense

Ephesians 6 outlines the spiritual weapons every believer is given:

1. Belt of Truth – Ground your life in God's Word.

2. Breastplate of Righteousness – Live in integrity and purity.

3. Gospel of Peace (Shoes) – Stand ready to share God's hope.

4. Shield of Faith – Block the fiery lies and attacks of the enemy.

5. Helmet of Salvation – Guard your mind with the assurance of God's grace.

6. Sword of the Spirit – Speak and apply Scripture boldly.

7. Prayer – Your constant line of communication with God.

"Put on the whole armour of God, that ye may be able to stand against the wiles of the devil." (Ephesians 6:11, KJV)

CHAPTER 8 PRACTICAL APPLICATIONS TO PROTECT THE SOUL IN SPIRITUAL WARFARE

◆ ◆ ◆

Biblical Applications:

1. Daily Put on the Armor of God – Pray through each piece (Ephesians 6:10–18).

2. Speak Scripture Aloud – Use God's Word as your weapon (Matthew 4:4–10).

3. Pray in the Spirit – Let the Holy Spirit guide your intercession (Romans 8:26).

4. Guard Your Inputs – Be mindful of what you watch, listen to, and absorb (Proverbs 4:23).

Medical & Scientific Applications:

1. Challenge Negative Thought Loops – Use truth to interrupt anxious patterns.

2. Use Visualization Techniques – Picture the armor of God as a method of spiritual focus and grounding.

3. Practice Daily Self-Reflection – Journaling thoughts and comparing them to Scripture strengthens emotional control.

4. Engage in Supportive Communities – Healthy spiritual environments promote mental and emotional resilience.

CHAPTER 9: DEATH, ETERNITY, AND THE SOUL'S FINAL DESTINATION

◆ ◆ ◆

One of the most critical aspects of spiritual health is understanding what lies beyond this life. Death is not the end—it is the beginning of eternity. The Bible is clear that every soul will live forever in one of two destinations: eternal life with God, or eternal separation from Him.

"And as it is appointed unto men once to die, but after this the judgment." (Hebrews 9:27, KJV)

Ignoring this truth leaves the soul vulnerable to fear, confusion, and deception. Embracing it brings peace, purpose, and hope.

What the Bible Says About the Afterlife

From Genesis to Revelation, the Bible teaches that the soul continues after death. Jesus Himself taught this repeatedly:

"In my Father's house are many mansions: if it were not so, I would have told you. I go to prepare a place for you." (John 14:2, KJV)

He also warned of the consequences of rejecting God:

"These shall go away into everlasting punishment: but the righteous into life eternal." (Matthew 25:46, KJV)

Heaven is a place of perfect communion with God. Hell is a place of separation, darkness, and judgment. The choice we make in this life determines our soul's final destination.

"For what is a man profited, if he shall gain the whole world, and lose his own soul?" (Matthew 16:26, KJV)

Scientific Accounts of Life After Death

While science cannot definitively prove the afterlife, there is growing interest in near-death experiences (NDEs). Thousands of people from various cultures and backgrounds report remarkably similar experiences:

Conscious awareness after clinical death

Encounters with a being of light

Life review

Overwhelming peace or terrifying fear

A sense of "returning" to finish a purpose

Prominent researchers, including cardiologists and neurosurgeons, have documented NDEs that cannot be explained by brain function alone. These accounts align with what Scripture says: the soul lives on.

A 2014 study published in Resuscitation documented over 2,000 cardiac arrest survivors. Many reported awareness during the time they were clinically dead, and some described vivid spiritual encounters.

These stories don't replace Scripture, but they do confirm what the Bible has always declared: there is life after death.

Living with Eternity in Mind

Knowing the truth about eternity changes how we live now. When you believe your soul is eternal, your priorities shift. You stop chasing temporary pleasures and start investing in things that last.

"Set your affection on things above, not on things on the earth." (Colossians 3:2, KJV)

A soul anchored in eternity lives with wisdom, urgency, and joy. Death loses its sting when your destination is secure.

"O death, where is thy sting? O grave, where is thy victory?… But thanks be to God, which giveth us the victory through our Lord Jesus Christ." (1 Corinthians 15:55, 57, KJV)

CHAPTER 9 PRACTICAL APPLICATIONS TO LIVE WITH AN ETERNAL PERSPECTIVE

♦ ♦ ♦

Biblical Applications:

1. Examine Your Salvation – Ensure your soul is right with God (2 Corinthians 13:5).

2. Store Up Eternal Treasures – Invest in God's Kingdom, not just worldly gain (Matthew 6:19–20).

3. Share the Gospel – Point others to eternal hope (Romans 10:14–15).

4. Live with Holy Purpose – Walk daily in light of your eternal calling (2 Timothy 4:7–8).

Medical & Scientific Applications:

1. Reflect on Mortality with Meaning – Studies show that healthy awareness of mortality increases life satisfaction.

2. Practice Legacy Thinking – Focusing on how your life impacts others improves emotional resilience.

3. Engage in End-of-Life Planning – Brings peace of mind and reduces stress for loved ones.

4. Use Mindfulness to Clarify Values – Meditating on eternal values promotes purpose-driven living.

CHAPTER 10: THE DANGERS OF BITTERNESS AND RESENTMENT

♦ ♦ ♦

Bitterness is like spiritual rust—it starts small, often hidden, but over time it corrodes everything it touches: joy, relationships, peace, and purpose. The Bible warns that bitterness is not just an emotion but a root that defiles the soul.

"Looking diligently lest any man fail of the grace of God; lest any root of bitterness springing up trouble you, and thereby many be defiled." (Hebrews 12:15, KJV)

Bitterness forms when pain is left unresolved, when forgiveness is withheld, and when offenses are allowed to fester. While anger may flare up in a moment, bitterness settles in over time—quietly poisoning your soul and damaging those around you.

Bitterness Blocks the Grace of God

Notice the warning in Hebrews: bitterness causes us to "fail of the grace of God." Why? Because bitterness hardens the heart and blinds us to God's mercy. When we dwell on how we've been wronged, we lose sight of how much we've been forgiven.

"And when ye stand praying, forgive, if ye have ought against any: that your Father also which is in heaven may forgive you your trespasses." (Mark 11:25, KJV)

Unforgiveness and bitterness block the flow of God's grace to us and through us. They trap us in a cycle of spiritual drought.

Scientific Consequences of Resentment

Bitterness doesn't just damage relationships—it damages your health. Studies have found:
Increased cortisol levels due to chronic anger and rumination

Higher risk of heart disease, hypertension, and immune dysfunction

Impaired sleep, concentration, and memory

Higher levels of depression and anxiety

A 2016 study published in Personality and Individual Differences confirmed that bitterness and long-term resentment are strong predictors of psychological distress. Another study from Hope College showed that participants asked to recall hurtful events with unforgiving thoughts experienced significantly higher blood pressure and heart rate.

The soul and body are connected—when the heart is poisoned by bitterness, the whole system suffers.

God's Cure: Letting Go

Scripture offers a powerful antidote to bitterness: grace.

"Let all bitterness, and wrath, and anger… be put away from you… And be ye kind one to another, tenderhearted, forgiving one another, even as God for Christ's sake hath forgiven you." (Ephesians 4:31–32, KJV)

Letting go is not denying the hurt—it's refusing to let it define you. Forgiveness is not about excusing wrongs but choosing freedom over captivity.

Bitterness says, "You owe me." Grace says, "God paid it." And healing begins.

CHAPTER 10 PRACTICAL APPLICATIONS TO UPROOT BITTERNESS

◆ ◆ ◆

Biblical Applications:

1. Forgive Freely and Often – Model Christ's example (Matthew 18:21–22).

2. Pray for Those Who Hurt You – Prayer softens resentment (Luke 6:28).

3. Release the Right to Retaliate – Trust God to handle justice (Romans 12:19).

4. Reflect on God's Mercy Toward You – Gratitude fuels grace (Psalm 103:10).

Medical & Scientific Applications:

1. Use Expressive Writing – Journaling about the hurt and choosing to forgive improves mental health.

2. Practice Reappraisal – Reframing the event from a broader perspective reduces emotional intensity.

3. Avoid Rumination Triggers – Set boundaries on people or environments that provoke bitterness.

4. Focus on Empathy and Compassion – Increases emotional flexibility and reduces chronic resentment.

CHAPTER 11: THE POWER OF HOPE AND PURPOSE

◆ ◆ ◆

Hope is one of the most vital forces in the human soul. It fuels endurance, lifts perspective, and gives meaning even in hardship. Without hope, the soul weakens. Without purpose, it drifts. God's Word teaches that both hope and purpose are not merely helpful—they are essential.

"For I know the thoughts that I think toward you, saith the LORD, thoughts of peace, and not of evil, to give you an expected end." (Jeremiah 29:11, KJV)

God has a plan. He offers not just comfort in suffering, but direction and destiny.

Biblical Hope is Anchored in God

Hope in the Bible is not wishful thinking—it's a confident expectation in God's faithfulness. It's a steady anchor in uncertain times.

"Which hope we have as an anchor of the soul, both sure and stedfast…" (Hebrews 6:19, KJV)

This kind of hope doesn't deny pain—it outlasts it. It doesn't depend on circumstances but on the unchanging character of God.

"Rejoicing in hope; patient in tribulation; continuing instant in prayer." (Romans 12:12, KJV)

In a world full of instability, God gives us something firm to hold onto: His promises.

Science Confirms: Hope Heals

Researchers have found that hope and a sense of purpose improve nearly every area of health:

A study in The Journal of Positive Psychology found that people with higher levels of hope reported lower levels of anxiety and depression.

Neuroscientists at the University of Michigan discovered that hope activates the brain's reward center, releasing dopamine—the "motivation molecule."

Purposeful living is linked to better sleep, stronger immune function, and even lower mortality rates (as shown in studies from The Lancet and JAMA Psychiatry).

In one study, elderly individuals who had a defined life purpose were 2.4 times more likely to avoid Alzheimer's disease. Hope literally strengthens the brain—and the soul.

Finding Your Purpose in God

The world often defines purpose by achievement, fame, or wealth. But the Bible defines purpose by identity in Christ and relationship with God.

"Thou art worthy, O Lord, to receive glory and honour and power: for thou hast created all things, and for thy pleasure they are and were created." (Revelation 4:11, KJV)

You were created on purpose, with purpose, for God's pleasure and glory. Your life matters—not because of what you do, but because of who made you and what He's doing through you.

CHAPTER 11 PRACTICAL APPLICATIONS TO CULTIVATE HOPE AND PURPOSE

◆ ◆ ◆

Biblical Applications:

1. Meditate on God's Promises – Remind yourself daily of His faithfulness (Lamentations 3:21–23).

2. Pray with Expectation – Speak to God about your purpose and future (James 1:5–6).

3. Serve Others in Love – Purpose grows when we focus outward (1 Peter 4:10).

4. Remember God's Calling on Your Life – You are His workmanship (Ephesians 2:10).

Medical & Scientific Applications:

1. Set Meaningful Goals – Purpose-driven people report higher life satisfaction and mental wellness.

2. Practice Visualization – Envisioning your future strengthens motivation and focus.

3. Volunteer in Aligned Areas – Doing work that reflects your values enhances mental clarity and emotional health.

4. Track Personal Growth – Journaling progress toward your goals reinforces hope and purpose.

CHAPTER 12: REST FOR THE SOUL – THE SABBATH AND SLEEP

◆ ◆ ◆

We live in a world that glorifies hustle and burns out the soul. Constant stimulation, overwork, and stress are treated as badges of honor—but God calls us to something radically different: rest. True soul health requires space to slow down, recharge, and reconnect with the One who made us.

"Remember the sabbath day, to keep it holy." (Exodus 20:8, KJV)

This wasn't just a suggestion—it was a command. One of the Ten Commandments. God, who needs no rest, modeled rest for us in creation and commanded it for our good.

The Sabbath: God's Gift of Rhythm

"And he said unto them, The sabbath was made for man, and not man for the sabbath." (Mark 2:27, KJV)

The Sabbath wasn't a religious burden—it was a spiritual gift. A day to rest, worship, reflect, and restore the soul. God knew that without regular rhythms of rest, the human spirit would collapse under the weight of life's demands.

Modern believers may not observe the Sabbath in a legalistic sense, but the principle remains: regular rest, worship, and disengagement from labor are essential for spiritual and emotional health.

Sleep: The Body's Spiritual Recharge

God designed sleep not only for the body—but also for the mind and soul.

"It is vain for you to rise up early, to sit up late… for so he giveth his beloved sleep." (Psalm 127:2, KJV)

Sleep is a divine gift, yet it is often the first thing we sacrifice. But studies are now confirming what Scripture declared all along: without rest, we unravel.

Chronic sleep deprivation is linked to anxiety, depression, reduced cognitive function, and emotional instability.

Deep sleep helps consolidate memory, regulate emotions, and remove toxic buildup from the brain.

A 2021 Harvard Medical School report confirmed that consistent sleep improves resilience, creativity, decision-making, and overall mental health.

When we push through life without adequate rest, we disconnect from the rhythms God designed to refresh the soul.

Jesus Modeled Rest

Even the Son of God rested. He withdrew from crowds, spent time in quiet places, and recharged with the Father.

"And he said unto them, Come ye yourselves apart into a desert place, and rest a while…"
(Mark 6:31, KJV)

If Jesus needed rest, how much more do we?

CHAPTER 12 PRACTICAL APPLICATIONS TO RESTORE THE SOUL THROUGH REST

◆ ◆ ◆

Biblical Applications:

1. Honor the Sabbath Principle – Set aside regular time to rest and worship (Isaiah 58:13–14).

2. Follow Jesus' Rhythm – Take breaks for solitude, reflection, and prayer (Luke 5:16).

3. Trust God to Work While You Rest – Let go of the need to control everything (Psalm 46:10).

4. Rest Without Guilt – God commands rest; it's not laziness—it's obedience (Hebrews 4:9–11).

Medical & Scientific Applications:

1. Maintain a Consistent Sleep Schedule – 7–9 hours supports emotional and cognitive health.

2. Create a Sleep-Friendly Environment – Reduce blue light, noise, and distractions before bed.

3. Take Strategic Rest Breaks – Short breaks throughout the day restore focus and reduce cortisol.

4. Practice Digital Sabbath – Disconnect from screens to reconnect with God and people.

CHAPTER 13: HUMILITY VS. PRIDE – THE MENTAL HEALTH CONSEQUENCES

◆ ◆ ◆

Few things affect the soul more powerfully than pride—or heal it more deeply than humility. While the world often exalts pride as confidence and self-assurance, the Bible consistently warns that pride leads to destruction. On the other hand, humility opens the door to wisdom, grace, and inner peace.

"Pride goeth before destruction, and an haughty spirit before a fall." (Proverbs 16:18, KJV)

"God resisteth the proud, but giveth grace unto the humble." (James 4:6, KJV)

Pride creates a barrier between us and God, between us and others, and even within ourselves. It causes us to defend our flaws, deny our need for help, and cling to control. Humility, however, acknowledges truth—and truth is the gateway to healing.

The Spiritual Root of Pride

Pride was the first sin—Satan's rebellion against God—and it remains at the root of many others.

Pride says:

"I don't need God."

"I'm better than others."

"I know best."

"I'll do it my way."

This attitude chokes out repentance, hardens the heart, and traps the soul in self-worship.

"The fear of the LORD is to hate evil: pride, and arrogancy, and the evil way…" (Proverbs 8:13, KJV)

But humility does the opposite—it softens, surrenders, and seeks truth.

"Humble yourselves therefore under the mighty hand of God, that he may exalt you in due time." (1 Peter 5:6, KJV)

Mental Health and the Burden of Pride

Pride doesn't just separate us from God—it also isolates us emotionally. Research shows that individuals who display high levels of narcissism or prideful defensiveness:

Struggle more with anxiety and relationship breakdowns

Have higher rates of emotional reactivity and depression

Are less likely to seek help or admit faults, delaying healing

Conversely, people who practice humility—marked by openness, teachability, and empathy—report:

Lower stress levels

Greater life satisfaction

Stronger relationships

Higher resilience in crisis

A 2016 study published in the Journal of Positive Psychology found that humility is positively associated with psychological well-being, forgiveness, and lower emotional volatility.

Humility not only honors God—it restores mental balance.

Jesus: The Ultimate Model of Humility

"Let this mind be in you, which was also in Christ Jesus: Who… made himself of no reputation, and took upon him the form of a servant… he humbled himself, and became obedient unto death, even the death of the cross." (Philippians 2:5–8, KJV)

Jesus, though sinless, humbled Himself to save us. When we follow His example, we lay down pride, embrace grace, and find true rest for our souls.

CHAPTER 13 PRACTICAL APPLICATIONS TO CULTIVATE HUMILITY AND DEFEAT PRIDE

♦ ♦ ♦

Biblical Applications:

1. Confess Sin Regularly – Pride hides sin; humility brings it into the light (1 John 1:9).

2. Submit to God's Will – Trust His way over your own (Proverbs 3:5–6).

3. Serve Others Without Recognition – True humility seeks no applause (Matthew 6:1–4).

4. Study the Life of Christ – Let His example shape your heart (John 13:12–17).

Medical & Scientific Applications:

1. Practice Active Listening – Listening to understand builds humility and empathy.

2. Invite Honest Feedback – Allows for personal growth and reduces blind spots.

3. Engage in Reflective Journaling – Writing about failures and lessons fosters self-awareness.

4. Admit When You're Wrong – Accepting responsibility reduces internal tension and improves emotional health.

CHAPTER 14: THE HEALING POWER OF SERVICE AND COMPASSION

◆ ◆ ◆

One of the greatest secrets to a healthy soul is this: stop looking inward and start looking outward. The world tells us to focus on ourselves—to chase personal fulfillment, comfort, and success. But Jesus taught the opposite: joy, healing, and purpose come when we serve others.

"Bear ye one another's burdens, and so fulfil the law of Christ." (Galatians 6:2, KJV)

Compassion is not weakness—it is spiritual strength. Service is not wasted energy—it is soul-deep medicine. When we align with God's heart for others, we find healing for ourselves.

Jesus: The Servant King

"Even as the Son of man came not to be ministered unto, but to minister, and to give his life a ransom for many." (Matthew 20:28, KJV)

Jesus, the King of kings, lived as a servant. He washed feet, fed the hungry, touched the outcast, and wept with the grieving. His life was love in action. He calls us to follow His example—not to earn salvation, but to live out the fruit of a transformed soul.

"By love serve one another." (Galatians 5:13, KJV)

Serving Others Heals the Server

Science now confirms what the Bible has taught all along: serving others is healing.

A study published in BMC Public Health found that volunteering is linked to lower levels of depression, higher self-esteem, and greater life satisfaction.

Neuroscientific research shows that acts of compassion activate the brain's reward center, releasing dopamine and oxytocin—the "feel-good" and "bonding" chemicals.

A 2020 report from Harvard Health concluded that people who regularly help others experience reduced stress, improved mood, and even longer lifespans.

When we take the focus off our own pain and pour into others, our own wounds begin to heal.

"If thou draw out thy soul to the hungry... then shall thy light rise in obscurity, and thy darkness be as the noonday." (Isaiah 58:10, KJV)

This isn't just spiritual poetry—it's practical truth. Helping others brings light into our own darkness.

Compassion as a Weapon Against Anxiety and Isolation

In a time when loneliness and anxiety are rampant, compassion breaks the cycle. Isolation tells us we are alone; service reminds us we're part of something bigger. Anxiety focuses inward; compassion shifts the focus outward.

"Let nothing be done through strife or vainglory; but in lowliness of mind let each esteem other better than themselves." (Philippians 2:3, KJV)

This mindset—thinking of others—guards the soul against pride, envy, and despair. And as we meet others' needs, God meets ours.

CHAPTER 14 PRACTICAL APPLICATIONS TO HEAL THROUGH SERVICE AND COMPASSION

◆ ◆ ◆

Biblical Applications:

1. Find a Way to Serve Weekly – Look for a need in your church, neighborhood, or home (Matthew 25:35–40).

2. Give Without Expecting in Return – Pure service reflects Christ (Luke 6:35).

3. Pray for a Heart of Compassion – Ask God to break your heart for what breaks His (Colossians 3:12).

4. Look for the Lonely – Be the hands and feet of Jesus to the hurting (James 1:27).

Medical & Scientific Applications:

1. Volunteer in an Area That Aligns With Your Values – Purpose-driven service improves emotional well-being.

2. Practice Small Acts of Kindness – Even brief moments of helping trigger mood-boosting chemicals.

3. Journal About the Impact of Helping – Reflecting on your service deepens its emotional and mental benefits.

4. Join a Service-Oriented Group – Community service boosts mental health through shared purpose.

CHAPTER 15: IDENTITY IN CHRIST VS. IDENTITY CRISIS

◆ ◆ ◆

In a world obsessed with self-expression, many are still searching for one foundational truth: Who am I? The soul longs for identity, but culture offers countless shifting labels based on performance, appearance, sexuality, career, or social status. The result is a generation caught in a crisis of identity—confused, anxious, and unstable.

"For we are his workmanship, created in Christ Jesus unto good works…" (Ephesians 2:10, KJV)

The Bible makes our identity clear. You are not an accident. You were handcrafted by a loving God, designed for a purpose, and redeemed through Christ.

The Dangers of a Shifting Identity

When your identity is based on something external—your job, relationship, looks, or success—it's fragile. If you lose it, you lose you. But the Bible offers a firm foundation.

"Therefore if any man be in Christ, he is a new creature: old things are passed away; behold, all things are become new." (2 Corinthians 5:17, KJV)

In Christ, your identity is not based on your past, your feelings, or others' opinions. It's based on His unchanging truth.

The Psychological Cost of Identity Confusion

Mental health professionals are sounding the alarm: identity instability is linked to numerous psychological challenges:

Depression

Anxiety

Borderline personality symptoms

Substance abuse

Low self-esteem

Suicidal thoughts

A 2020 study in the Journal of Affective Disorders found that identity confusion is a significant predictor of emotional dysregulation and mental distress. Conversely, people with a secure sense of self are more emotionally resilient and less vulnerable to peer pressure or destructive behavior.

Christ Restores a Broken Identity

The enemy attacks the soul by distorting identity. He whispers lies like:

"You're worthless."

"You'll never change."

"You are what you've done."

"You'll never be loved."

But God speaks a better word:

"Ye are a chosen generation, a royal priesthood, an holy nation, a peculiar people…" (1 Peter 2:9, KJV)

"There is therefore now no condemnation to them which are in Christ Jesus…" (Romans 8:1, KJV)

The more you meditate on your identity in Christ, the more stable, peaceful, and focused your soul becomes.

CHAPTER 15 PRACTICAL APPLICATIONS TO ROOT IDENTITY IN CHRIST

♦ ♦ ♦

Biblical Applications:

1. Declare Who You Are in Christ – Speak the truth of Scripture over yourself (Ephesians 1:3–14).

2. Replace Lies with Truth – Identify false beliefs and combat them with God's Word (John 8:32).

3. Read and Reflect on Your Adoption as God's Child – Let His love redefine you (Romans 8:15–17).

4. Surround Yourself with People Who See You Through God's Eyes – Healthy community affirms true identity (Hebrews 10:24–25).

Medical & Scientific Applications:

1. Create an "Identity Statement" – Write out who you are beyond roles and titles; read it daily.

2. Practice Grounding Techniques – Remind yourself of unchanging truths during anxiety episodes.

3. Limit Social Media Exposure – Reduces comparison and identity confusion.

4. Engage in Purposeful Activities – Doing what aligns with your values reinforces authentic identity.

CHAPTER 16: THE WEIGHT OF SHAME VS. THE FREEDOM OF GRACE

♦ ♦ ♦

Shame is one of the heaviest burdens the soul can carry. Unlike guilt, which says "I did something wrong," shame whispers, "I am something wrong." It isolates, condemns, and hides. It keeps people stuck in cycles of sin, fear, and emotional paralysis. But the Bible offers a powerful solution—grace.

"Whosoever believeth on him shall not be ashamed." (Romans 10:11, KJV)

God never designed us to live under shame. His desire is to cover us— not in fear or condemnation, but in mercy, love, and righteousness.

Shame Enters in the Garden

Shame is as old as humanity. The first time it appeared was immediately after sin:

"And the eyes of them both were opened… and they knew that they were naked; and they sewed fig leaves together…" (Genesis 3:7, KJV)

Before sin, Adam and Eve were naked and unashamed (Genesis 2:25). After sin, shame rushed in—and they hid. That is still what shame does: it causes people to hide from God, others, and even themselves.

But God came searching. And He still does today.

Grace Lifts Shame

"There is therefore now no condemnation to them which are in Christ Jesus…" (Romans 8:1, KJV)

Condemnation is the language of shame. Grace speaks a better word. When you surrender to Christ, your sins are forgiven and your shame is removed.

"As far as the east is from the west, so far hath he removed our transgressions from us." (Psalm 103:12, KJV)

Through Jesus, the soul can walk in freedom—not because you've earned it, but because God offers it. Grace transforms the identity of the ashamed into the beloved.

The Psychological Effects of Shame

Modern psychology confirms that unresolved shame is toxic to mental health:

It is linked to depression, anxiety, addiction, and PTSD.

It impairs self-worth and leads to isolation.

It often fuels perfectionism, self-harm, and suicidal thoughts.

A study published in Psychology and Psychotherapy (2017) found that high levels of internalized shame correlate strongly with psychological distress and emotional dysregulation.

But healing is possible—and it begins when shame is brought into the light.

Confession, Grace, and Restoration

The Bible doesn't hide the failures of its heroes. David, Peter, Paul—they all battled shame. But through confession and God's grace, they were restored.

"He restoreth my soul…" (Psalm 23:3, KJV)

Healing comes when we stop running and start receiving—God's forgiveness, love, and new beginning.

CHAPTER 16 PRACTICAL APPLICATIONS TO BREAK FREE FROM SHAME

◆ ◆ ◆

Biblical Applications:

1. Confess and Receive Forgiveness – Bring shame into the light (1 John 1:9).

2. Meditate on God's Grace – Let His mercy replace your self-condemnation (Titus 3:5–7).

3. Reject Condemning Thoughts – Recognize the enemy's lies and replace them with truth (2 Corinthians 10:5).

4. Accept Your New Identity in Christ – You are not what you've done; you are who God says you are (Isaiah 61:7).

Medical & Scientific Applications:

1. Use Cognitive Reframing – Challenge shame-based thoughts with truth and compassion.

2. Practice Self-Compassion – Treat yourself with the kindness you would extend to others.

3. Join a Safe Support Group – Sharing your story in a healthy environment reduces shame.

4. Engage in Restorative Practices – Activities like prayer, journaling, art, and counseling can reprocess and release toxic shame.

CHAPTER 17: THE HEALING POWER OF CONFESSION AND HONESTY

♦ ♦ ♦

Biblical Insight:

Confession is one of the most powerful, yet underused tools for spiritual health. The Bible repeatedly emphasizes the importance of confessing sin—not to shame us, but to free us.

"He that covereth his sins shall not prosper: but whoso confesseth and forsaketh them shall have mercy." (Proverbs 28:13, KJV)

"Confess your faults one to another, and pray one for another, that ye may be healed." (James 5:16, KJV)

Honesty with God and others breaks the grip of shame, lifts the weight of secrecy, and opens the door to healing. It's not weakness—it's surrender, and surrender is where the soul finds strength.

Scientific Connection:

Modern therapy practices, such as talk therapy and narrative therapy, are built on the premise that verbalizing what is hidden—especially guilt, trauma, or sin—reduces psychological distress.

A 2018 study in JAMA Psychiatry found that open disclosure in therapy reduced symptoms of depression and anxiety more effectively than cognitive therapy alone.
Confession-type practices also decrease activity in the amygdala (the brain's fear center), increasing emotional regulation and clarity.

The soul was not meant to carry secrets—it was meant to be transparent before God and honest with others.

CHAPTER 17 PRACTICAL APPLICATIONS TO FREE THE SOUL THROUGH CONFESSION

❖ ❖ ❖

Biblical Applications:

Practice daily confession in prayer (1 John 1:9)

Confess to a trusted, godly person for accountability (Galatians 6:1–2)

Examine your heart regularly in the presence of God (Psalm 139:23–24)

Medical & Scientific Applications:

Try journaling your inner struggles and naming what you feel

Participate in group therapy or a support group

Use guided reflection exercises to identify and release guilt or unresolved emotions

CHAPTER 18: THE STRENGTH FOUND IN SURRENDER AND TRUST

♦ ♦ ♦

Biblical Insight:

In a culture that idolizes control and self-reliance, God calls us to something countercultural—surrender. The soul is not meant to carry every burden, solve every problem, or control every outcome. True spiritual strength is found when we let go and trust God fully.

"Trust in the LORD with all thine heart; and lean not unto thine own understanding." (Proverbs 3:5, KJV)

"Casting all your care upon him; for he careth for you."
(1 Peter 5:7, KJV)

Surrender is not defeat—it is rest. It's the only way the soul can be truly at peace.

Scientific Connection:

The attempt to control everything is a major driver of anxiety and burnout. Studies show that people who develop what psychologists call "trust-based coping" or "faith-based surrender" experience:

Lower stress hormones (cortisol)

Improved sleep quality

Increased emotional resilience

Stronger sense of peace and purpose

A 2021 study in The Journal of Health Psychology concluded that people who surrendered control in faith-based practices had significantly lower stress levels and greater life satisfaction.

CHAPTER 18 PRACTICAL APPLICATIONS TO STRENGTHEN THE SOUL THROUGH SURRENDER

◆ ◆ ◆

Biblical Applications:

Pray prayers of surrender daily (Luke 22:42)

Meditate on God's sovereignty (Psalm 46:10)

Release outcomes to God and focus on obedience over results (Matthew 6:33)

Medical & Scientific Applications:

Practice "letting go" meditation techniques

Journal what you can and cannot control—then release what isn't yours

Use breathing techniques alongside prayer to reinforce surrender

CHAPTER 19: THE PEACE THAT COMES FROM OBEDIENCE

♦ ♦ ♦

Biblical Insight:

Obedience is often misunderstood as restrictive, but in God's design, obedience leads to peace, clarity, and freedom. The soul thrives when it aligns with God's will—not out of legalism, but love.

"Great peace have they which love thy law: and nothing shall offend them." (Psalm 119:165, KJV)

Obedience protects the soul from chaos. God's commandments are not burdens—they are boundaries that guard us from harm and guide us toward life.

"If ye know these things, happy are ye if ye do them." (John 13:17, KJV)

Obeying God—even when it's difficult—produces spiritual maturity, emotional stability, and a clear conscience.

Scientific Connection:

Studies show that living in alignment with one's core values produces:

Reduced cognitive dissonance (the stress of living against what you believe)

Increased psychological well-being

Higher life satisfaction and moral confidence

A study published in The Journal of Positive Psychology found that individuals who live by consistent moral convictions experience greater peace of mind, fewer regrets, and stronger resilience in decision-making.

Obedience to God aligns your soul with eternal truth—and that brings deep, lasting peace.

CHAPTER 19 PRACTICAL APPLICATIONS TO ANCHOR THE SOUL THROUGH OBEDIENCE

◆ ◆ ◆

Biblical Applications:

Read and reflect on God's commandments regularly (Psalm 1:1–3)

Ask the Holy Spirit for strength to obey (John 14:26)

Repent quickly when you fall short and return to God's ways (Isaiah 55:7)

Medical & Scientific Applications:

Practice value-clarity journaling: identify where your actions match or conflict with your beliefs

Use accountability systems to stay aligned with your convictions

Reduce decision fatigue by living with moral consistency

CHAPTER 20: THE SOUL'S NEED FOR WONDER AND WORSHIP

◆ ◆ ◆

Biblical Insight:

The soul was created to worship. When we lose our sense of awe for God, we begin to drift into spiritual apathy, emptiness, or idolatry. Worship realigns the soul with its Creator, lifting our eyes from the world's chaos to heaven's glory.

"O come, let us worship and bow down: let us kneel before the LORD our maker." (Psalm 95:6, KJV)

"Thou art worthy, O Lord, to receive glory and honour and power…" (Revelation 4:11, KJV)

Wonder softens the heart. Worship nourishes the soul. Together, they bring joy, humility, and perspective.

Scientific Connection:

Psychologists and neuroscientists now recognize the therapeutic value of awe and beauty. Studies show that moments of wonder:

Reduce inflammation and stress markers

Increase compassion and generosity

Promote emotional regulation and connectedness
Trigger the release of oxytocin, dopamine, and serotonin

One 2015 study in Emotion found that experiencing awe—even from nature or art—leads to greater well-being and humility. These findings mirror what the Bible teaches: the soul needs wonder to stay spiritually alive.

CHAPTER 20 PRACTICAL APPLICATIONS TO AWAKEN THE SOUL THROUGH WORSHIP AND AWE

◆ ◆ ◆

Biblical Applications:

Set aside time for daily worship (Psalm 100:1–4)

Reflect on God's creation, character, and works (Psalm 8:3–4)

Praise God even in trials—worship brings breakthrough (Acts 16:25–26)

Medical & Scientific Applications:

Spend time in awe-inspiring environments (nature, stargazing, music)

Practice intentional gratitude during worship—magnifies mental health benefits

Use music therapy or sound healing in conjunction with prayer

CONCLUSION: ALIGNING WITH GOD'S BLUEPRINT FOR SPIRITUAL HEALTH

♦ ♦ ♦

Throughout this book, we've explored the deep wisdom of the Bible concerning the soul—how it functions, what harms it, and how it can be healed. At every turn, we've seen how modern science is finally beginning to confirm what Scripture has declared for thousands of years. The alignment between biblical truth and medical discovery is not coincidence —it is evidence of divine authorship.

How could ancient authors, writing without modern psychology or neuroscience, understand that prayer restructures the brain… that gratitude rewires emotional response… that forgiveness restores health… that shame devastates mental well-being… and that community, purpose, worship, and rest are essential for flourishing?

They knew—because God knew.

"All scripture is given by inspiration of God…" (2 Timothy 3:16, KJV)

The Bible is not just a religious text—it is the Creator's guide for human thriving. Every command, every promise, every principle has been given by a loving God who designed the soul and knows exactly how it flourishes.

But this book is about more than wellness. Its deeper purpose is not simply to help you live well—but to help you live forever. God didn't give us the Bible just to help us navigate stress, anxiety, or confusion. He gave us His Word to reveal Himself—to show us the way to salvation through His Son, Jesus Christ.

True spiritual health begins with a relationship with God. And that relationship only comes through the grace made available at the cross.

You were not made to struggle alone. You were made to walk with God—whole, healed, forgiven, and free.

CALL TO FAITH: A PERSONAL INVITATION TO RECEIVE JESUS CHRIST

◆ ◆ ◆

If you've read this far, it means you care about your soul—and that is no accident. The God who created you has been pursuing you with His love from the very beginning. Everything in this book, every truth and insight, leads to this moment: the opportunity to be made new in Jesus Christ.

The greatest need of the soul is not peace, purpose, or clarity. The greatest need is salvation.

"For all have sinned, and come short of the glory of God." (Romans 3:23, KJV)

"For the wages of sin is death; but the gift of God is eternal life through Jesus Christ our Lord." (Romans 6:23, KJV)

Every human being has sinned. And sin separates us from God—not just in this life, but for eternity. But God, in His mercy, made a way. He sent His Son, Jesus, to take our place on the cross, to pay the debt of our sin, and to rise again in victory—so that we might live.

"But God commendeth his love toward us, in that, while we were yet sinners, Christ died for us." (Romans 5:8, KJV)

"That if thou shalt confess with thy mouth the Lord Jesus, and shalt believe in thine heart that God hath raised him from the dead, thou shalt be saved." (Romans 10:9, KJV)

Salvation is not earned by religion, good works, or spiritual discipline. It is a free gift, received by faith.

SALVATION PRAYER

♦ ♦ ♦

If you've never received Jesus as your Savior—or if you're unsure where you stand—you can make that decision right now. This simple prayer is not magic, but if it reflects your sincere heart, God will hear and respond:

"Heavenly Father, I know that I am a sinner. I believe Jesus died for my sins and rose again. I ask You to forgive me, cleanse me, and make me new. I turn from my old ways and put my trust in Jesus Christ alone. I confess Him as my Lord and Savior. Come into my heart and fill me with Your Holy Spirit. From this day forward, I want to live for You. Thank You for saving me. In Jesus' name, Amen."

If you prayed that prayer and meant it, welcome to the family of God. Your soul has been redeemed, your past forgiven, and your eternity secured. Now, begin walking in the blueprint God has laid out for your soul—and never walk alone again.

SUPPORT THIS MINISTRY

♦ ♦ ♦

We would love to connect with you! If this book has impacted you, or if you want to learn more about Jesus, discipleship, or getting plugged into a community, we're here to help.

Get the Word to the World is a nonprofit outreach ministry funded entirely by donations. Our mission is to put Bibles in the hands of men, women, and children who don't have one.

You can follow our Facebook page at:

[Get the World to the World](#)

ABOUT THE AUTHOR

Jordan Schneider

Jordan Schneider is a devoted father to a beautiful little boy and passionate follower of Jesus Christ. Although he grew up in church and was familiar with the teachings of the Bible, his life was forever changed in 2022 when he experienced a radical transformation through divine intervention. Since that moment, Jordan has commited his life fully to Chrit and is sharing the truth of God's Word.

He holds an Associate's Degree in Biblical Studies and a Bachelor's Degree in Theology. With a heart for teaching and a deep love for Scripture, Jordan seeks to bridge biblical truth with practical living. He also has a strong passion for fitness and healthy living which he often integrates into his biblical teachings to help others care for both body and soul. His writing reflects his desire to see others experience the life-changing power of God's Word in every area of their lives.

BOOKS BY THIS AUTHOR

God's Blueprint For Health: How The Bible Knows Your Body

God's Blueprint for Health reveals how ancient biblical widson aligns with modern science to promote true health. From clean eating and fasting to mental wellness and disease prevention, this book shows how God's word offers a complete guide to caring for your body-just as He designed. It's where faith meets fitness for a life of strength, purpose, and Godly living.

God's Blueprint For Mental Health: How The Bible Knows Your Body

God's Blueprint for Mental Health reveals how the Bible—written thousands of years ago—offers powerful, practical solutions for anxiety, depression, trauma, and more. Blending timeless Scripture (KJV) with modern psychological insights, this book shows that the Creator of your mind also gave you the manual to heal it. Discover peace, clarity, and purpose through God's original design for mental wellness.

God's Blueprint For Spiritual Health: How The Bible Knows Your Soul

God's Blueprint for Spiritual Health uncovers how the Bible holds the timeless keys to healing the soul. Backed by modern science, this book shows how Scripture leads to lasting peace, purpose, and restoration.

God's Blueprint For Overcoming Temptation: Winning The War Against Your Flesh

God's Blueprint for Overcoming Temptation equips believers to conquer lust, lies, addiction, pride, and more using biblical truth and scientific insight. With practical strategies and spiritual wisdom, this book shows how to break free from the grip of sin and walk in lasting victory through the power of God's Word and Spirit.

Made in the USA
Coppell, TX
25 April 2025